KEW'S
BIG TREES
SECOND EDITION

CHRISTINA HARRISON

Kew Publishing
Royal Botanic Gardens, Kew

CONTENTS

INTRODUCTION

He who plants a tree loves others besides himself –
ENGLISH PROVERB

In our hearts we know that trees are important.
To some they are green monuments or emerald
cathedrals that augment our landscape and bewitch
us with their folklore, while to others they are vital for
survival, providing shade, food, fuel and medicine.
Britain's own history is entangled with the oak,
yew, juniper, ash and other trees that clothe our
countryside, and it was not so long ago that we used
them for everything from weapons to water carriers.
There are also plenty of places where ancient trees
are still found as markers of boundaries, people and
events long gone; living testaments to the memories
of previous generations.

Today we remain dependent on these impressive
woody plants; they provide vital green spaces for us
to relax in and reduce the temperature on our busy
streets. Trees continuously provide oxygen and soak
up carbon dioxide, provide life-saving medicines,
fibres for clothing, fruit for eating (and drinking),
dyes, resins, spices, latex, and of course timber for
everything from cricket bats to Venetian blinds, musical
instruments, and even the paper you are reading this
from. They are integral to our lives.

At the Royal Botanic Gardens, Kew, we care for
thousands of trees, collected from around the world.
Together they are an invaluable living encyclopaedia
and a precious resource for conservation.

The English oak (*Quercus robur*) is perhaps the best known of our
native tree species and is entwined with our history and folklore.

A WORLD OF DIVERSITY

The wonder is that we can see these trees and not wonder more – **RALPH WALDO EMERSON**

There are thought to be between 60,000 and 80,000 species of tree in the world; a definite number is not yet known, and new species are described every year. Most species occur in the tropics, with temperate regions such as the UK having only a small percentage of the total. Tree species are amazingly diverse, ranging from those that tower hundreds of feet into the sky to the diminutive specimens of the windswept tundra. There are trees that can live for 5,000 years, while others rarely live to over a hundred; there are species that can live partly submerged in water for large parts of their lives, while others survive in hot, arid conditions.

Trees are not just a wonder in themselves; they are home to hundreds of other species and together create habitats that nurture wildlife, understorey plants, fungi and insects. Amazingly, tree canopies are said to be home to at least 50 per cent of all species on our planet. This is just one of the reasons why deforestation can be so devastating. Today, woodland covers around 13 per cent of the UK, half of which is deciduous broad-leaved woodland and half coniferous forest. It has been estimated that there are around 3.8 billion trees in this country, and although this may sound a lot, in reality we have less than half the percentage of other European countries such as France, Spain and Italy. However, the woodland habitat is one that many of us in this country value more than any other; one that creates a sense of well-being and fires our imaginations.

At the Royal Botanic Gardens, Kew you can discover a world-class, historic collection of trees. There are around 14,000 trees here, of more than 2,000 species and varieties. Over 300 of these are Champion Trees (the largest of their kind in the country) including the chestnut-leaved oak (*Quercus castaneifolia*) and the lacebark pine (*Pinus bungeana*) near the Waterlily House, a *Cotinus obovatus* near Victoria Gate and a *Magnolia campbellii* not far from the Children's Garden.

OPPOSITE: Trees support many other species and together create an important habitat for other plants including bluebells, wild garlic, primroses and ferns.

BELOW: Seek out Kew's magnolia collection in spring and you'll find many impressive specimens in full flower, including the glorious *M. campbellii*.

THE STORY OF KEW'S TREES

There is something nobly simple and pure in a taste for the cultivation of forest trees – **WASHINGTON IRVING**

Kew is a world-renowned 'botanic garden'. This means that many of the plants here have been collected from natural sources (or 'the wild'), and are kept in collections, often planted in groups that are related to each other. This allows Kew's scientists to easily find and compare plants and use them in their research. The Arboretum at Kew is a comprehensive collection of hardy trees that stretches over most of the 132 hectares (326 acres) of the Gardens. However, it was not always so leafy here.

When King George II and Queen Caroline took up residence on the Richmond estate along the River Thames in 1721 they employed the most fashionable garden designer of the day, Charles Bridgeman, to transform the grounds from open farmland to a royal landscape garden. Bridgeman planted many beeches and elms, oaks and horse chestnuts to create a sylvan landscape. Although none of his work remains, there are several elderly sweet chestnuts (*Castanea sativa*) close to the Lake that date from around this period. They are believed to have either been part of the boundaries to the ornamental fields and wildernesses that he designed, or of plantings that edged the Richmond estate along what was then a road called Love Lane. A stately English oak (*Quercus robur*), now a memorial tree near the head of the Lake, is also thought to date from this time.

The adjoining Kew estate was leased in 1731 by George II's son, Frederick, Prince of Wales, who began to landscape the grounds in earnest. This was a time of many new plant introductions, with new trees and shrubs being sent from the far-flung corners of the globe. There was a great new interest in botany that ran alongside the emergence of the English Landscape Movement, and many new landscaped estates and gardens such as Painshill and Stowe were being created. Plant and seed importers such as Peter Collinson and John Bartram provided the species that furnished many of these estates and several new plant nurseries started around this time. Receipts still exist of Frederick's purchases of trees from nurseries such as the one that once existed on Kew Green that was run by Richard Butt. He supplied some of the first trees to Kew, and in all provided £1,000 worth of trees for Frederick. After Frederick's untimely death in 1751, his wife, Princess Augusta, continued his work, and with the help of her friend Lord Bute founded a nine-acre botanic garden next to the Orangery in 1759. Five acres of this were set aside to be an arboretum of special trees. Specimens dating from this period that you can still visit include the maidenhair tree (*Ginkgo biloba*), black locust tree (*Robinia pseudoacacia*) and Japanese pagoda tree (*Styphnolobium japonicum*) that all grow near to the Princess of Wales Conservatory, and the large oriental

CLOCKWISE FROM TOP LEFT: Take in the formal planted vistas, Treetop Walkway, planting around the Lake, Kew's Natural Areas, and the oak collection to get a sense of the variety of temperate trees grown in the Gardens.

plane (*Platanus orientalis*) next to the Orangery. These are now known as Kew's Old Lions. It is thought many of these trees came from the Duke of Argyll's estate in Whitton. The Duke, Bute's uncle, was an avid tree collector and had many botanical rarities. By 1768, there were 488 hardy trees and shrubs growing at Kew, and by 1789 there were 630. It soon out-shone many other gardens for its number of species and its rarities.

George III joined the Kew and Richmond estates in 1802, and added many new plant species under the guidance of naturalist and explorer Sir Joseph Banks. After the King's death the Gardens became the responsibility of the government, and William Hooker was appointed Kew's first director in 1841. He worked tirelessly to expand the collections. Land that had previously remained part of the Royal Pleasure Grounds was eventually given to Hooker to create an Arboretum worthy of the botanic garden of a proud nation. William Andrews Nesfield was hired to landscape the grounds and organise the Arboretum into groups of trees related to each other. He laid out vistas and avenues that centred on the newly constructed Palm House to lead visitors out into the Gardens. In 1870, William Hooker's son, Joseph, the second director at Kew, set out the plans for a pinetum (conifer collection) in the south of the Gardens. This replaced an original collection near Elizabeth Gate and a small pinetum that existed next to the Palm House (some older specimens of which can still be seen there). It was under Joseph that the Arboretum took its present-day shape.

The early nineteenth century was an era of frenzied conifer collecting, with many new introductions brought into the country by the famous plant hunter David Douglas. Notable trees introduced in this era included sitka spruce (*Picea sitchensis*) in 1831, Monterey cypress (*Cupressus macrocarpa*) in 1838, coast redwood (*Sequoia sempervirens*) in 1843, and giant redwood (*Sequoiadendron giganteum*) in 1853. Many tree avenues were also planted at Kew in the late nineteenth century, including the Hawthorn Avenue (1868), Acacia Avenue (1872), Holly Walk (1874) and the Sweet Chestnut Avenue (1880). You can still stroll down Holly Walk today.

Change continued throughout the twentieth century: the major pine collections were transferred to Bedgebury in Kent, which had been selected as the site for a new national pinetum, while other collections such as birch (*Betula*) and southern beech (*Nothofagus*) went to Wakehurst in West Sussex (Kew's sister garden) to benefit from the cleaner air. Kew also began collaborating with Castle Howard in Yorkshire where more specimens of select species could be planted. Kew continued to take part in expeditions overseas to expand the collections, while new curation techniques improved their quality. A skilled arboricultural unit now ensures that all the trees remain in good condition, with pioneering plant health techniques alongside an extensive tree management database.

The severe storms of October 1987 and January 1990 had a major impact on the Arboretum at Kew. Nearly 700 trees were lost in total, primarily mature broad-leaved deciduous trees from the areas developed under William Hooker. Head of the Arboretum, Tony Kirkham, decided not to rush to replant but to take time to assess the collections as a whole and see exactly how they could be improved and how planting techniques could prevent such losses happening again. The collections have since expanded due to carefully planned collecting trips, and the main vistas have benefited greatly from replanting work.

Kew now has many enviable collections including that of the genus *Quercus* (oak) of which, between the Kew and Wakehurst sites, there are over 2,874 specimens of 128 taxa. Such wonderful collections sit perfectly in the heritage landscape setting and can be enjoyed by both visitor and botanist alike.

The Mediterranean Garden near King William's Temple includes many species that in previous decades would not have thrived at Kew, including the olive (*Olea europaea*). Many gardens in the UK, especially in the south-east, can now support plants from hotter, drier regions and this garden focuses on this change of climate.

Kew's tree collections face many problems in this new century, including new pests and diseases from other countries, droughts, storms and soil compaction. The Arboretum team works to combat all of these and also continues to expand and complete these important collections. You can now visit the headquarters of the Arboretum (not far from the Sackler Crossing) and see the work of the teams employed here. This amazing assemblage of trees, tucked into a wonderful green space near one of world's busiest cities, is truly unique. Now a UNESCO World Heritage Site with collections of global significance, Kew is rich in history and breathtaking beauty in every season.

BELOW: Many impressive cedars now grace the Gardens, from those around the Palm House and Orangery to those near the Great Pagoda and along Cedar Vista.

WALK AMONG GIANTS

The best friend on Earth of man is the tree. When we use the tree respectfully and economically, we have one of the greatest resources of the Earth – **FRANK LLOYD WRIGHT**

The Arboretum stretches over the majority of the Gardens, but if you don't have time to see it all here are some of the highlights. The grid references provided link to the Gardens' visitor map and should help you locate some of these beautiful specimens.

If you enter the Gardens through Victoria Gate you can enjoy a host of beautiful, ornamental specimens as soon as you arrive. Look out for the sawtooth oak (*Quercus acutissima*) right near the entrance, as well as a fine *Cotinus obovatus* near the Temple of Bellona (J9). Walk past the Palm House Pond (L8) and you'll see some fantastic examples of swamp cypress (*Taxodium distichum*), which is one of only a handful of deciduous conifers. If you head to the Woodland Garden (N8) you'll find some wonderful understorey and ground plantings, rhododendrons, a handkerchief tree (*Davidia involucrata*), witch hazels (*Hamamelis*), *Edgeworthia* and magnolias, as well as two unusual Chinese nettle trees (*Celtis sinensis*) and an old black walnut (*Juglans nigra*).

Stroll along the Broad Walk (N6) and you can discover an avenue of impressive Atlas cedars (*Cedrus atlantica*), colourful *Liquidambar styraciflua*, a matching pair of tulip trees (*Liriodendron tulipifera*) and a large purple beech (*Fagus sylvatica f. purpurea*). Near the Orangery are two Wollemi pines (*Wollemia nobilis*) – a species that was thought extinct only 30 years ago, one was planted by Sir David Attenborough, the other by Prince Philip, Duke of Edinburgh. Nearby there is an old cucumber tree (*Magnolia acuminata*) and a gnarly old black locust tree (*Robinia pseudoacacia*) (P6), which despite their age still flower every year.

Near the Secluded Garden (P6) you'll find Kew's famous maidenhair tree (*Ginkgo biloba*), which is one the nation's '50 Great British Trees' and is also one of Kew's Old Lions (the oldest trees in the Gardens), planted in 1762. The nearby reclining specimen of the Japanese pagoda tree (*Styphnolobium japonicum*) is also a fascinating Old Lion planted in 1760.

Heading south towards the Temperate House you can find the maple (*Acer*) collection (G9). This is a must-see in autumn when the reds, golds, oranges and yellows of the leaves create a magical and photogenic scene. Near the Great Pagoda is the Japanese Gateway (C8), and here you'll also find fiery maples as well as shagbark hickories (*Carya ovata*), which turn a shining gold in autumn.

In the Woodland Glade (E5) near the Lily Pond on Cedar Vista, among the hydrangeas and rhododendrons you'll find plenty of interesting trees such as the Japanese snowbell (*Styrax japonicus*), the empress tree (*Paulownia tomentosa*), and *Emmenopterys henryi* and *Litsea cubeba* from China. This spot is well worth a visit at any time of year especially as the Redwood Grove (D5) is just a step

RIGHT: A stroll along the Broad Walk offers many beautiful sights, including a pair of stately tulip trees, which have tulip-like flowers in summer and turn a rich gold in autumn.

away where you can experience the majesty of these Californian giants and see a stone circle on the path showing just how big they can grow.

In Kew's Natural Areas (B3) around Queen's Charlotte's Cottage you can enjoy a much more natural woodland experience with plenty of native trees and woodland flowers. Here the woodland is managed sustainably – dead wood is left to stand, hazel is coppiced in a seven-year cycle and wildlife is encouraged. Make sure you take a stroll along the boarded Woodland Walk (B2) to see the best of this area.

A walk around the Lake (G4), taking in the Sackler Crossing and Syon Vista, is a great way to enjoy a whole variety of trees and shrubs, including swamp cypress (*Taxodium distichum*) and an ancient English oak (*Quercus robur*) complete with its own tree seat. At the head of the Lake, near the Mediterranean Garden (H7), you will also discover some of the Gardens' oldest inhabitants – a collection of sweet chestnuts (*Castanea sativa*) with swirling, twisting bark. One of these was used to make a mould for the Whomping Willow in the Harry Potter films. The chestnut nearest King William's Temple is believed to be the oldest tree in the Gardens, dating from the early 1700s. Inside the Mediterranean Garden you can discover olive trees (*Olea europaea*), stone pines (*Pinus pinea*), cork oaks (*Quercus suber*) and a half-reclining Judas tree (*Cercis siliquastrum*) that puts on a mass of purple-pink flowers every May, followed by rich purple pods and vibrant autumn foliage.

If you walk from the Mediterranean Garden towards the Children's Garden, you'll find a newly planted area of flowering cherries and colourful maples on your left (K5). Here you can also meet a towering tulip tree (*Liriodendron tulipifera*), some rare Chinese tulip trees (*Liriodendron chinense*), and the large, beautifully domed *Carpinus betulus* 'Fastigiata'. Head into the nearby magnolia collection (K4) in spring and you can spend time among their blousy pink, white and yellow blooms, with species such as the magnificent *Magnolia campbellii* putting on a sumptuous display.

The oak collection is always well worth a visit too (I1). In autumn, look out for the northern red oak (*Quercus rubra*) and the pin oak (*Quercus palustris*) among the many species here between Brentford Gate and along Riverside Walk. In fact, every inch of the Gardens offers some new delight and you can't fail to discover fascinating trees in whatever direction you stroll. In the following pages we cover some of Kew's most impressive trees, but in reality, they are all important and interesting in their own right.

DID YOU KNOW?

It is thought that around 10,000 species of trees (around 16 per cent) are threatened with extinction. Kew works around the world with key partners in 110 countries to discover, describe and conserve trees and other plants for the benefit of everyone. See **kew.org** for more information.

BELOW, LEFT: The twisting ridged bark of a sweet chestnut is a sure sign of its age.

OPPOSITE: Kew is home to many ash species, including this European ash *(Fraxinus excelsior)*. The is one of several native species now under threat from new pests and diseases.

JAPANESE PAGODA TREE

Styphnolobium japonicum

One of Kew's Old Lions, this twisted old heritage tree dates back to 1760 and is one of the few remaining trees from the original nine-acre botanic garden on this site (O6).

It was one of five specimens imported from China by James Gordon (a famous nurseryman of the day) who introduced the species to the UK in 1753. This specimen is thought to be one of the first to be planted in the UK; others were planted near the Great Pagoda (C9) later on.

Although named the Japanese pagoda tree, this species is from the temperate woodlands of China. It is thought to have been given its common name of pagoda tree due to the fact it is often found planted near Buddhist temples. It is widely grown as an ornamental due to its hanging inflorescences (flowering spikes) of creamy-white flowers. In Japan, its durable wood was used for pillars and door frames, while in China, extracts of the leaves, flowers and fruits are used in traditional medicine. A yellow dye can be extracted from the flowers or seedpods, which is commonly used for silks and batik.

This tree is a piece of living history in other ways too as it shows a record of arboricultural techniques: many ways have been used to support its remaining branches over the years while the brick wall around its base protects an aerial root. Its two remaining almost horizontal trunks are what is left of a much larger, more upright tree.

The species was re-named in early 2006 after its DNA was examined and its true relationships to other species was discovered. Previously known as *Sophora japonica* it is now more correctly known as *Styphnolobium japonicum*. Kew's scientists have studied this plant's chemistry and its use in the cosmetics industry.

INSET: The distinctively shaped flowers give away which plant family this tree belongs to – Fabaceae, the pea family.

OPPOSITE AND BELOW: This beautiful flowering tree is an Old Lion and one of the most iconic trees in the Gardens.

MAIDENHAIR TREE

Ginkgo biloba

Maidenhair trees are the only surviving members of an ancient group of plants that were widespread at the same time as the dinosaurs. This species was first introduced to Europe from China via Japan around 1730. As well as being handsome trees they are botanically very interesting as they were once placed in the same family as the yew (Taxaceae) but are now separated from the conifers and placed in an order all of their own, the Ginkgoales, of which this species is the only living representative.

Revered in eastern China, where only a few still grow wild in mountainous regions, you can find many ancient specimens planted around temples. The common name of maidenhair tree comes from the shape of its leaves, which are similar to that of the maidenhair fern, while the name *Ginkgo* is believed to be a Japanese derivation of the Chinese word *yin-kuo* meaning silver fruit. Ginkgos have separate male and female trees (they are dioecious). The males have cone-like pollen-bearing flowers while female trees produce the rather pungent apricot-like fruits. In China the seeds are used in medicines to treat digestive problems, hangovers and asthma, while leaf extracts are used for circulatory problems. There are claims that it can improve memory, and several trials have also studied whether ginkgo extracts may alleviate some symptoms of dementia, or help people recover from a stroke, although there is currently little good evidence to support this.

The oldest *Ginkgo biloba* at Kew (P6) was grown by James Gordon of Mile End nurseries in 1758, having been introduced to the UK by him in 1754. It is thought to have been planted around 1762. Old accounts recall the tree being grown against the wall of the Great Stove (a glasshouse built in 1761 for Princess Augusta) where it was trained 'like a fruit tree'. This specimen may easily have been one of the first planted in this country, while several others were planted in the Gardens in 1773. This is a male tree and is particularly beautiful in autumn when its leaves turn a bright golden yellow. In 2002 it became one of the 50 'Great British Trees' in a scheme run by the Tree Council for the Queen's Golden Jubilee. It is also a Champion Tree, meaning that it is the largest of its kind in the country.

INSET: The large edible seeds of the *Ginkgo* are found inside its yellowish fruits, known for their foul smell.

LEFT: Mature leaves are fan-shaped and two-lobed, turning a beautiful buttery yellow in autumn.

OPPOSITE: Kew's *Ginkgo* is one of 50 Great British Trees and also a Champion Tree.

CHESTNUT-LEAVED OAK

Quercus castaneifolia

This handsome oak (L6) is native to the mountainous region between the Black and Caspian Sea known as the Caucasus, as well as being found in the Alborz mountains of Iran. It has never been widely planted in this country, even in botanical collections, so Kew's specimens are particularly valuable. In appearance it looks very similar to the Turkey oak (*Q. cerris*), which is common throughout Europe. Clothed in shining dark-green leaves for most of the year, this species produces good-sized acorns that are flushed with orange at the base and sit within bristly cups. Though bitter they are often eaten by jays, squirrels and other wildlife.

The chestnut-leaved oak was introduced to the UK as seed in 1843 and it was from this first batch that Kew's trees were grown. This specimen was planted in 1846 not long after 45 acres of new land was given to Kew to extend the Arboretum. Today it is one of the finest trees in the whole of Kew and is a Champion Tree measuring over 35 m tall and 35 m spread. In fact, it is the biggest, finest specimen known of its type. But this is not its only claim to fame as it is also the fastest-growing tree in the Gardens and the largest.

INSET: The leaves of this species resemble those of a sweet chestnut but the typical acorns sit in large bristly cups.

ABOVE: Although this tree has lost a couple of large limbs in recent years, its huge canopy remains extremely impressive.

OPPOSITE: This enormous stately specimen tree is the largest of its kind in the country.

BLACK LOCUST TREE

Robinia pseudoacacia

This beautiful member of the bean family (Leguminosae) is adorned with feathery green foliage and hanging racemes of incredibly fragrant white flowers every summer. Native to Virginia and the eastern USA, it is thought to have been introduced to this country around 1634 by the famous plant hunter John Tradescant and his son. The tree's hard, heavy timber is resistant to decay, and it was originally hoped that it would prove a valuable timber tree here. Its trunk wood however was found to be nowhere near as strong as English oak (see p 48). It was therefore mainly used for dowels and 'tree-pins' to hold timbers together in shipbuilding. In May and June, the tree bears racemes of pretty creamy-white flowers. In its native America this tree is a major food source for honeybees that produce a delicious 'acacia' honey. In autumn you'll find the tree adorned with long narrow seedpods.

This old gnarled specimen (P6) was planted in 1762 and by 1768 there were three species of *Robinia* growing at Kew. The spot where it grows marks the site of Kew's first small arboretum, and here it grew next to a Turkey oak (*Quercus cerris*), a cedar of Lebanon (*Cedrus libani*), a cork oak (*Quercus suber*) and an American locust tree (*Diospyrus virginiana*), all of which were well regarded. Most of the trees originally planted in this area were from an estate in Whitton that belonged to the Duke of Argyll, a famous and pioneering tree collector of his day. Although now in decline, this tree has recently been rejuvenated by careful cultivation and continues to grow and flower.

ABOVE: This *Robinia* was one of the first trees to be planted in Princess Augusta's new arboretum in 1762.

OPPOSITE: This ancient-looking tree has been strengthened with the help of metal bands around its trunk.

TURNER'S OAK

Quercus x turneri

This hybrid oak is a huge dark dome of a tree. It is unusual for being semi-deciduous, meaning that it keeps its foliage throughout the winter. Its dark-green lobed leaves have wavy edges and only turn brown and fall once the new leaves appear in spring. It is believed to have been raised around 1783 by Spencer Turner at the Holloway Down Nursery in Essex, as a cross between holm oak (*Q. ilex*) and English oak (*Q. robur*). However, it was not properly named until 1880. Planted in the original small arboretum at Kew in 1798, little is otherwise known of its history other than this must have been one of the original batch of saplings grown by Turner. Natural crosses of the two parent trees are rare so propagation of this hybrid is best achieved by grafting semi-ripe cuttings and several new trees have been grown at Kew this way.

Now a large sturdy specimen, Kew's Turner's oak (O6) was the inspiration for a new technique of caring for mature and heritage trees in the Gardens. In 1987 during the Great Storm the tree and its roots were literally lifted up by the winds and then dropped. When it settled back into the ground the tree had a new lease of life. It was surmised that the soil had been de-compacted by this lifting, allowing the tree to access more water and nutrients, helping it to grow better. Today, older trees in the Gardens have the soil around their roots injected with compressed air to reduce de-compaction and increase their lifespan.

LEFT: This semi-deciduous tree has multiple large low-growing branches, creating a huge domed canopy.

OPPOSITE: This tree inspired a whole new way of reviving older trees at Kew, and continues to grow every year.

LUCOMBE OAK

Quercus x *hispanica* 'Lucombeana'

The Lucombe oak (J6) is also a hybrid semi-deciduous tree that is a cross between the deciduous Turkey oak (*Q. cerris*) and the evergreen cork oak (*Q. suber*). It was discovered in 1762 by William Lucombe, an Exeter nursery man, who noticed a very vigorous seedling growing among his Turkey oak seedlings close to a cork oak. The seedling had reached a height of seven metres in only seven years. It was in fact a natural hybrid of the two trees and is known to occur in the wild. Lucombe propagated it in large numbers by grafting – in this instance onto an English oak rootstock.

At maturity the Lucombe oak is a very stately tree, reaching 30 m in height. Like the Turkey oak, it has corrugated bark and a trunk buttressed at the base. Its smooth, bright green leaves have a grey downy under-surface, and can stay on the tree for most of the winter.

Although the tree produces fertile acorns, the plants grown from them vary considerably between the cork and Turkey oaks, so the hybrid is best propagated by grafting or budding.

The impressive specimen at Kew is believed to date from the time when this hybrid was first discovered and must have been one of the first to have been bought from Lucombe. It was planted out in what was then known as the Pleasure Grounds. In 1846, when this tree was already a large mature specimen, it was lifted and moved 20 metres to allow a new avenue of holm oaks (*Quercus ilex*) to extend from the Palm House to the River Thames (now Syon Vista) according to new plans for the Arboretum laid out by the landscape designer William Andrews Nesfield. The move was completed successfully and the tree continues to thrive.

FAR LEFT: It is reputed that William Lucombe later felled his original tree to provide wood for his own coffin and kept the boards under his bed.

LEFT: The Lucombe oak was winched out of place and replanted using oxen, but later Kew used the more efficient 'Barron's tree transplanter' to move mature trees.

STONE PINE

Pinus pinea

Stone pines or umbrella pines are native to southern Europe, particularly the Iberian Peninsula, and large forests can be found in Spain, Portugal and Italy. They have been grown in the UK and Europe for many centuries for their pine nuts, but it was not until 1846 that Kew planted its first specimen. This particular tree (P7) can still be found at the entrance to the Secluded Garden and is immediately recognisable by its large multi-branched tilted growing habit, and thick plates of red-brown bark. It is a landmark tree at Kew, is held in great affection, and is one that many visitors recognise on a return trip to the Gardens.

Kew's stone pine was one of the first trees to be planted out in the newly extended Arboretum when William Hooker became director of Kew in the nineteenth century. Many conifers in the north end of the Gardens date from this time. The fact that this tree originally sat for many years as a potted plant in the nursery before being planted may account for its unusual shape. In the wild, stone pines have straight, tall trunks with an umbrella of foliage on top. Their thick bark is deeply fissured into broad vertical plates, which gives the species a special architectural quality. Recently, two large branches had to be removed from this tree due to storm damage, and although this altered its beautiful habit it is hoped this work will prolong the tree's life as much as possible.

RIGHT: Stone pines have a canopy of short grey-green needles. They produce large round cones, which contain edible pine nuts.

ABOVE: The thick red-brown bark of this tree makes it easily recognisable. It is also known as the umbrella pine or parasol pine.

PINE NUTS

Around 20 species of pine produce edible nuts large enough to be worth harvesting. In Europe they have been eaten for many hundreds of years and are vital ingredients in a wealth of well-known dishes, and sauces such as pesto. They can also be pressed to extract an oil, which is said to be packed with antioxidants.

SWEET CHESTNUT
Castanea sativa

Reputedly one of the trees brought to Britain by the Romans, the sweet chestnut is today one of this country's most beloved landscape trees. Native to southern Europe, where many old and fabled specimens are still to be found, they have long been valued for their edible starchy brown nuts. These trees have also been used for boundary markers, fencing and hop poles, for making charcoal, flour and porridge, and to provide food for pigs. Their distinctive twisting ridged bark, glossy leaves and spiky fruits make this a favourite tree with many people. They have been planted in large numbers over the centuries especially in deer parks and landscape gardens.

There are several old sweet chestnuts at Kew, some of which are believed to be remnants of an avenue of trees that once ran along the boundary of Love Lane (the road that divided Kew into its two original royal estates). These characterful trees can be found near the head of the Lake (H6). You can discover the sweet chestnut that has the distinction of being the oldest tree at Kew, with its immense gnarled and colourful trunk, near King William's Temple (I7), opposite a drinking fountain. We ask that should you visit this tree you treat it with the utmost respect. It has, after all, been around since the early eighteenth century, seen nine monarchs on the throne and survived bombing raids during the Second World War!

LEFT: One of the old sweet chestnuts near the head of the Lake was used as a mould to make the bark for the Whomping Willow in the Harry Potter films.

OPPOSITE: The oldest tree at Kew is this beautiful stout sweet chestnut near the entrance to the Mediterranean Garden.

PLANE TREES

Platanus orientalis and x *hispanica*

The oriental plane (*Platanus orientalis*) is believed to have been brought to England from south-eastern Europe around 1562, although it could have been even earlier. It has long been regarded as a stately parkland tree and can achieve a great age. It has attractive dappled bark, deeply-lobed leaves and round bristly fruits that dangle, like baubles, from the branches, making this an easy tree to recognise.

An immense and beautiful specimen stands near the Orangery (O4) that was once part of a line of three trees that joined the edge of this building to a royal palace that once stood nearby. Called the White House, this palace was the home of Prince Frederick and Princess Augusta (founder of the botanic gardens). It is generally believed that this tree came from an estate in Whitton that was owned by the prodigious tree collector the Duke of Argyll. Argyll's nephew, Lord Bute, spent much of his time helping Frederick and Augusta furnish their grounds with interesting plants. Bute brought many trees from Whitton to Kew in 1762 after his uncle died and his estate was sold off. Today, this tree is known as one of Kew's Old Lions and receives specialist care as a heritage tree.

You can also see several impressive London planes (*Platanus* x *hispanica*) at Kew. These are actually hybrids of the oriental plane and American sycamore (*Platanus occidentalis*), and although much more common are considered to be less beautiful than

RIGHT: This lovely old oriental plane near the Orangery and Kew Palace dates from the eighteenth century.

ABOVE: You can easily recognise a plane tree by its dangling spherical fruits.

their parents. First described in 1663, they are great city trees as they can shed their bark in small plates thereby removing any pollution and allowing their bark to continue to breathe. It has been estimated that 50 per cent of London's trees are in fact London planes. At Kew there is an immense specimen in the Rhododendron Dell (J2) that may have been planted by the famous landscape designer Lancelot 'Capability' Brown in the eighteenth century. Another specimen exists at the end of the Broad Walk near the Palm House Pond (M7), and there is also one near the Ice House (N6). One of the finest London planes in the country can be found along the river not far from Kew, near Richmond Bridge.

CORSICAN PINE

Pinus nigra subsp. *laricio*

Native to the western Mediterranean, the Corsican pine, with its rough grey bark and bright green needles, can be found in large numbers throughout Corsica, Calabria and Sicily. A subspecies of the much more common *Pinus nigra* (Austrian or European black pine), the Corsican pine is extensively grown in the Mediterranean as a forestry tree and can grow in a wide range of soils and climates. It is thought to have been introduced to the UK around 1788.

Kew's oldest Corsican pine stands tall and proud in an area of meadow by Elizabeth Gate (Q5). Planted in 1814, it was brought to Kew as a six-inch seedling by the botanist R.A. Salisbury, from the south of France, and is said to be the oldest specimen in the country. It stands as a living representation of the position of Kew's original pinetum, which held 36 species. Over the years this tall tree has suffered a few misfortunes, including being struck by lightning twice and also by a small light aircraft in 1928, leading to it being dubbed Kew's unluckiest tree. This species produces copious amounts of resin, and this can set alight when trees are hit by lightning; trees have been known to literally explode when this happens. The resin has been put to many uses over the centuries but today is mainly harvested for 'rosin' for rubbing on horsehair bows for violins and cellos.

Many ornamental conifers were planted in the original botanic garden here, but most did not fare well. This tree is one of the few survivors, along with the stone pine (see p28).

ABOVE: The tall straight trunk is typical of the Corsican pine and makes it a perfect forestry tree.

OPPOSITE: Kew's Corsican pine is around 30 m tall; it would be taller but its top was taken off when it was struck by a light aircraft in 1928!

TULIP TREES

Liriodendron tulipifera and *chinense*

There are just two species of tulip tree and you can see fine examples of both at Kew. The North American tulip tree (*Liriodendron tulipifera*) was introduced to the UK sometime in the mid-seventeenth century and was one of the first plant introductions from that continent. This fast-growing forest species is native to eastern North America and is valued for its timber. Tulip trees grow to be large and beautiful specimens, with distinctive lobed leaves that unfold as they mature from within a protective pair of leaf scales. Their extraordinary greenish flowers resemble a tulip and give this species its common name and its deserved reputation as a wonderful ornamental tree. They are also known as important 'honey plants' in the USA.

Near the magnolia collection at Kew, you can discover a stately old specimen that was planted in the 1770s and is now over 30 m tall (J4). There are also several younger tulip trees nearby, but these are in fact Chinese tulip trees (*L. chinense*), which were introduced to this country by the plant hunter Ernest Wilson in 1901. Chinese tulip trees are native to southern and central China, and are very similar to the American species, but are much rarer due to habitat loss in the wild. You can easily tell the difference between the two species when they flower as *L. tulipera* have bright orange markings on their flowers while the smaller *L. chinense* flowers do not.

In 1996 Kew mounted an expedition to the Daba Shan in Sichuan, China, and collected seeds from a single specimen of *L. chinense* found in primary forest. The seed produced only a handful of young trees, so the Kew team revisited the area in 1999 and, using the 1996 GPS co-ordinates, found the exact same tree standing alone with most of the surrounding large trees felled for timber. It alone had been retained because its height was perfect for a skyline to extract timber to the roadside. Ironically, the stress placed on it by its use as an anchor had produced large quantities of good seed. Twenty-eight young trees were grown from these seeds and planted at Kew in 2001 to recreate the Arboretum's old Tulip Tree avenue (J4). Very few wild-source Chinese tulip trees are known in cultivation, so these trees are valuable for both research and conservation of the species.

INSET: Be sure to seek out Kew's tulip trees in autumn when their leaves turn a shining golden yellow.

OPPOSITE: Kew's largest North American tulip tree was planted around 1770 and is now 30 m tall.

ABOVE: You can tell the two species of tulip tree apart when they flower – the North American tulip tree has bright orange markings on its larger flowers (see top), while the Chinese tulip tree has smaller greenish flowers (below).

CEDARS

Cedrus libani, atlantica and *deodara*

Once revered by ancient peoples in the Holy Land, the cedar of Lebanon (*C. libani*) can grow to become an immense tree that exudes a power all of its own. It is mentioned many times in the Bible as a symbol of might and beauty, and because of the strength and fragrance of its wood. These cedars were famously used for the building of King Solomon's Temple in Jerusalem.

Native to Lebanon, Syria and the Taurus Mountains in Turkey, cedar of Lebanon was introduced to the UK in the mid-seventeenth century and became very popular as a stately tree for landscaped gardens in the eighteenth century. While the trees in the ancient groves on Mount Lebanon are believed to be around a thousand years old, the oldest specimens at Kew date from when the Gardens were first landscaped in the mid-eighteenth century.

You can see many cedars in the Gardens – there are several near Victoria Gate and around the Palm House. Head for the Great Pagoda (C9) to see a fine specimen of a cedar of Lebanon. This tree slightly spoils the view, but it was once one of a grove of cedars here, planted around the time when the Pagoda was completed in 1762. It was such a fine specimen when Pagoda Vista

INSET: The seed cones of the Atlas cedar turn from a beautiful pale green to a rusty brown as they mature.

was created that no-one wanted to remove it. From here head down Cedar Vista (D6) (planted in 1871) to see a mix of Atlas (*Cedrus atlantica*) and deodar (*Cedrus deodara*) cedars. You can also enjoy several large, spreading Atlas cedars along the Broad Walk (N6).

These wonderfully impressive and evocative trees are now sadly under threat in their native habitat from deforestation, grazing, pests and climate change, and restoration measures are proving necessary to ensure they do not disappear forever. The remaining groves on Mount Lebanon were declared a UNESCO World Heritage Site in 1998.

BELOW: Take a stroll along Cedar Vista to enjoy the beauty of these majestic trees.

MONKEY PUZZLE

Araucaria araucana

One of the most curious trees that we know and love is the monkey puzzle, familiar to us because of the over-sized specimens we often see in people's front gardens. In the wild these trees are an awe-inspiring sight; a vision of a prehistoric landscape. Fossils of this species have been found that date from the Jurassic period, proving that they have survived unchanged since the time of the dinosaurs.

An evergreen conifer native to Argentina and Chile, this tree's Latin name is derived from Arauco, the name of the Chilean province where the tree was first found. It was first revealed to Europeans around 1780 when described by a Spanish explorer, and was introduced to the UK by Archibald Menzies in 1795, after which it soon became a status symbol to own one. Menzies was a plant collector and naval surgeon on Captain George Vancouver's circumnavigation of the globe travelling in Captain Cook's old ship HMS *Discovery*. He was served the seeds of this conifer as a dessert while dining with the governor of Chile. Instead of eating them, he later sowed them, returning home to England with five healthy plants. One of these could be seen growing at Kew until 1892.

Monkey puzzles can live to be ancient trees and can grow to 50 m tall. When young they have a pyramid shape with branches down to the ground (see the specimen near the Orangery at P5), but once they reach maturity at around 100 years old they begin to lose their lower limbs until they have a distinct high canopy of branches balanced on a straight grey trunk. Head to the grove of monkey puzzles near the Lake at G5 to see a mixture of young and mature specimens. Their distinctive tough, spiky triangular leaves are arranged in spirals, and this complex arrangement is thought to be how the tree came by the common name of 'monkey puzzler' in the nineteenth century.

This species has separate male and female trees, each producing a different-shaped cone. Male trees can be distinguished by the smaller pollen cones that hang down from the branches, while the females hold their large round cones upright. These female cones produce a wealth of seeds that are food for many birds and animals as well as people. The ancient Pehuenche people of Chile have a strong link with the monkey puzzle and consider it sacred; they have long been campaigning to try to halt its demise in the wild.

LEFT AND FAR LEFT: The monkey puzzle tree with its spiky triangular leaves and drooping branches has a very distinctive shape. Look out for a grove of them near Kew's Lake.

WOLLEMI PINE

Wollemia nobilis

One of the world's oldest and rarest living tree species, the Wollemi pine is a bit of a celebrity in the plant world. It was only discovered in 1994 and has been in the spotlight ever since. This species was known from fossil records of 90 million years ago but was presumed extinct until National Park Officer David Noble spotted it in a remote gorge in the Blue Mountains outside Sydney, Australia. It was the botanical find of the century!

Wollemi pines are related to the monkey puzzle (see p 40) and Norfolk Island pine in the family Araucariaceae. They are quite distinctive with drooping branches and bark that looks like bubbling chocolate. They grow to an impressive size: the tallest and oldest trees in the wild are 40 m high and believed to be around a thousand years old. There are less than 100 individuals known in the wild, but since its discovery a conservation strategy has been put in place that includes mass propagation of the tree, with the aim that with Wollemi pines available to everyone the wild trees would be safe from plant collectors. The Wollemi pine recovery plan set up by Wollemi Australia and Kew has ensured the continued survival of this amazing

INSET: Wollemi pines have narrow pendent male reproductive cones, which produce the pollen. By contrast the round female cones are held upright.

LEFT AND ABOVE: Sir David Attenborough planted the first Wollemi pine in the public part of the Gardens in 2005. It has now grown considerably into a very healthy tree.

ancient species. Kew carried out the UK hardiness trials in secret locations before the tree went on general sale to ensure it could survive British winters. There was no need to worry – all the trees thrived and continue to grow at a rapid rate.

You can see two Wollemi pines near the Orangery (P5) – one that was planted by Sir David Attenborough in 2005 and another planted by the Duke of Edinburgh in 2009 to mark Kew's 250th anniversary. You can also see a small grove of these trees near the Davies Exploration House (F7), one of which was planted by David Noble in 2010. Wollemi pines have grown so well since being planted at Kew that a new generation has already been raised from seed gathered from the original specimens.

HANDKERCHIEF TREE

Davidia involucrata

A beautiful tree with an ethereal quality, the handkerchief tree has heart-shaped mid-green leaves and unusual pure-white flower bracts, making it a wonderful addition to any garden.

The showy bracts (which can be up to 30 cm long) appear in early summer and hang in rows along the branches. They flutter delicately in the breeze, giving rise to this tree's common names of handkerchief tree, ghost tree and dove tree. Between each pair of bracts is a globe of reddish flowers held on drooping stalks consisting of many tiny dark male flowers and one or two longer female flowers. Spherical, ridged fruits develop from the flowers and turn brown when ripe; they contain a single hard nut that is packed with seed.

Introduced in 1903 and 1904 by the famous plant hunter Ernest Wilson from south-west China, this species was actually named after the man who first discovered and described it in 1869, Father Armand David. This Franciscan missionary and keen plant-lover spent most of his life in China. Wilson said of this tree, 'To my mind *Davidia involucrata* is at once the most interesting and beautiful of all trees of the north-temperate flora', and there are not many who would disagree.

Davidia have been grown at Kew since their first introductions. You can find several examples at Kew – near Princess Walk (K5), the Waterlily House (L6), and the Woodland Garden (N8). They are best seen in May when they are in full flower.

OPPOSITE: Head to the Woodland Garden to see a fine specimen of a handkerchief tree along the main path.

RIGHT: The white bracts that surround the flowers hang down from the branches and put on a spectacular display in May.

GUM TREES

Eucalyptus

Gum trees are immensely diverse and can be quite a puzzle for the taxonomist with each species being quite varied in itself depending on where it grows. Kew and Wakehurst hold around 39 species of this wonderfully evocative tree genus. You can see some fine examples around the Aquatic Garden (P8), including *Eucalyptus dalrympleana* or the mountain white gum. Native to south-eastern Australia and Tasmania, this fast-growing species can grow to around 20 m high in perfect conditions. This mighty specimen was only planted in 1972 and is already approximately 18 m high. You can see why you shouldn't plant one in a small back garden. The other specimens here are the black gum (*Eucalyptus aggregata*), an equally tall specimen, the snow gum with its ghostly white stems (*E. pauciflora*), and the spinning gum (*E. perriniana*). These are all great examples of the ornamental attributes of gum trees, which are valued for their white- and cinnamon-coloured trunks, with their bark hanging in ribbons and their grey-green leaves rustling in the merest breath of wind. Standing underneath these evergreen trees you can close your eyes, take in their distinctive scent and be reminded of the Antipodes. The scent comes from an oil inside the leaves, and this oil has long been used as a natural antiseptic and decongestant, and its medicinal potential continues to be studied.

The foliage of gum trees is intriguing as the young leaves are round and have their bases wrapped around the stem, but after time they are replaced with very different stalked, narrow and elongated leaves. Small white frothy flowers appear throughout the summer and once pollinated turn into neat little woody capsules that hold the seeds.

REACH FOR THE SKY

It is thought that the tallest tree ever recorded in the world was a *Eucalyptus regnans* or Australian mountain ash. It was measured in 1872 at 133 m (436 ft) high and was named the Ferguson Tree after the man who measured it, William Ferguson. The current record holder is a coast redwood (*Sequoia sempervirens*) in California, called Hyperion, which measures 116 m high (380 ft).

LEFT: Most gum tree species produce masses of pretty frothy white flowers all along their stems.

OPPOSITE: You can enjoy several impressive *Eucalyptus* species around the Aquatic Garden near the Princess of Wales Conservatory.

ENGLISH OAK

Quercus robur

Oaks hold a special place in our hearts. They are a part of British culture: used for their timber and bark, as boundary markers, memorial trees and as a symbol of strength and fertility. The oldest English oak at Kew, which stands near the head of the Lake (H4), is an immense individual and has stood here proud and strong for around 300 years. It is fitting then that this noble tree is dedicated to the memory of the crew of Pan Am Flight 103 who lost their lives in the Lockerbie disaster of 1988. Kew was possibly one of the last places that passengers and crew would have seen before rising above the clouds as they left Heathrow airport.

It is believed that this tree is one of the original trees planted by eighteenth-century garden designer Charles Bridgeman when this part of the Gardens was the royal Richmond estate belonging to King George II and Queen Caroline. Bridgeman planted many native trees, elms and sweet chestnuts as he landscaped the grounds.

Oaks are home to astonishing amounts of wildlife. In fact, they are home to more species than any other tree in the UK. Hundreds of invertebrate species are dependent on oak trees while many more species of

INSET: The distinctive lobed oak leaf has been used throughout our history and culture as a symbol of strength and knowledge.

ABOVE AND LEFT: The old English oak near the Lake is a very special memorial tree and the perfect place for quiet contemplation.

bird, bat, fungi, lichen, moss, fern and other plants are reliant on the habitat they create as woodland. The English oak is one of only two native species of oak in this country, the other being the sessile oak (*Quercus petraea*), which can be differentiated from the English oak in a number of ways including the fact that their acorns do not have stalks while English oak acorns do.

Kew's impressive oak collection can be found along the riverside path (I1) from Brentford Gate towards the top of Syon Vista. This is a real treat in autumn when the flame reds, amber hues and dusky browns of the leaves can be enjoyed to the full.

SAPPHIRE DRAGON TREE

Paulownia

Paulownia is a little-known genus of deciduous trees from China and eastern Asia. Although you may not be familiar with them you cannot fail to be impressed when you finally encounter them. With leaves the size of dinner plates, flowers similar to foxgloves and unusual pointed fruits that contain thousands of small winged seeds, these are trees that once met are not easily forgotten.

Paulownia are extremely fast-growing trees and in some countries are grown purely for their timber. In China they are used for reforestation programmes and roadside planting because they grow well in practically any soil. *Paulownia* wood is also famous for its use in making musical instruments, carvings, and more recently, surfboards. They are often also grown as pollarded specimens in flower borders for their architectural leaves.

Two large *Paulownia fargesii* can be found along Camellia Walk near the Berberis Dell (19). You will pick them out easily by their large, thick, slightly downy leaves. Native to China, this species was first sent to Kew in 1908 and first flowered here in 1928. It seems to fare better in this country than other *Paulownia* species.

A large *Paulownia tomentosa* (or foxglove tree) can be found near the Woodland Glade (E6). This species is also known as the empress or princess tree in Japan where traditionally a specimen was planted when a baby girl was born; its pale wood was then used to make a dresser for her dowry when she married. As with other *Paulownia* the flowers appear in spring from buds that have over-wintered on the branches. The long panicles of tubular purple and yellow flowers are a wonderful sight and usually appear in May if the buds have not suffered frost damage. It is said that there are few more beautiful flowering trees than this species.

The *Paulownia kawakami* (or sapphire dragon tree) behind the Waterlily House is a truly special individual. This rare tree was grown from seed collected by the head of Kew's Arboretum Tony Kirkham during a collecting trip to Taiwan in 1992 and was the first of its species to be planted at Kew in 1995. This species grows up to 12 m high and has blousy lilac flowers.

LEFT: The flowers of *Paulownia kawakami* have beautiful markings inside the delicate lilac petals.

OPPOSITE: In May look out for the foxglove tree in full flower as you approach the Woodland Glade, off Cedar Vista.

BLACK WALNUT

Juglans nigra

One of Kew's finest old black walnuts, believed to have been planted in the eighteenth century, can be found in the middle of the Woodland Garden (N8). Introduced to Europe in the early seventeenth century, this species is native to North America and eastern Canada. Its common name comes from its dark brown timber and bark, as well as the nuts it produces. The bark is deeply furrowed on its tall straight trunk, which holds a spreading crown of long pinnate leaves. Each of the leaflets is pointed, toothed and slightly downy underneath, and they are notable for releasing a scent when crushed.

The black walnut has separate male and female flowers which appear in May, and the male catkins can be up to 10 cm long. Once pollinated the female flowers develop into spherical fruits that ripen in October. Black walnut fruits are much harder to break into than the common walnut, and have a strong flavour, so don't tend to be harvested for their nuts. The wood however is highly valued for its beautiful dark colour and is often used in high-quality furniture and veneers. It has also long been used for making gunstocks, and during the First World War it was also used for aeroplane propellers due to its strength and durability. First Nation peoples in North America have also long used the black walnut in traditional medicine.

The fruits, leaves and roots contain a variety of active compounds, including juglone, which it has been suggested can act as a natural herbicide on certain plants around the base of the tree (allelopathy), and may also deter pests. However, you'll see that plenty of other plants grow here. In spring you'll also notice some intriguing violet flowers appearing around the base of this particular tree. These are not crocus, but the parasitic purple toothwort (*Lathraea clandestina*). These hooded claw-like leafless flowers are living off the roots of the tree, stealing nutrients but not causing it any harm.

OPPOSITE: Make a special trip to see Kew's old black walnut in the Woodland Garden as autumn begins to turn its leaves a golden yellow.

BELOW: The spherical fruits of this walnut species are not easy to get into and only contain small hard seeds.

BEECH

Fagus sylvatica 'Purpurea' and 'Pendula'

Take a stroll along the Broad Walk at Kew and you'll see two very different but entirely related beech trees with interesting tales to tell. You'll find one majestic specimen near the main path (N6) next to the Hive. Complete with characteristic smooth grey-green bark and a vast dome of wine-coloured leaves, this is of course the purple beech. In 1766, botanist Dr John Hope, on a visit to Kew, noted down many of the fine trees in Princess Augusta's original botanic garden, including 'a purple beech from Germany'. It is possible that this tree is the very same specimen, but there is currently no evidence to confirm this, so it may have been planted in the mid-1800s as part of William Hooker's extension of the Arboretum. Purple beeches are a natural variant of the common beech, their oval leaves being a purple or coppery colour and fringed with delicate hairs. They are a popular choice in large landscape gardens to add colour and variety.

Nearby, close to the Ice House (M7), you'll see a vast spreading weeping beech, which has also been dubbed 'the walking beech' as some of its branches have rooted into the soil and in turn become a ring of new trunks helping the tree advance outwards. The weeping beech is also a natural variant of the common beech. It has green leaves but an unusual habit, with large drooping and sometimes undulating branches. Viewed from a distance this tree forms a strange angular lumpy form, but step underneath its canopy in summer, and you'll be enveloped in its verdant beauty. Thought to have been planted as part of the development of the Arboretum in the 1840s by William

ABOVE: Look out for the purple beech along the Broad Walk with its vast dark dome of leaves.

LEFT: The weeping beech with its waving undulating branches has real character – see if you can see the face on its trunk!

Hooker it is now one of the most characterful trees in the Gardens.

Beeches do well at Kew as they like the light, well-drained soil. You can see another impressive purple beech near the Ruined Arch (F10), and you can find other stately beeches throughout the Gardens as well as in the Natural Areas (B3).

FURTHER READING

What we are doing to the forests of the world is but a mirror reflection of what we are doing to ourselves and one another – **MOHANDAS KARAMCHAND GANDHI**

Desmond, Ray. (2007)
The History of the Royal Botanic Gardens, Kew.
ROYAL BOTANIC GARDENS, KEW

Flanagan, Mark, Kirkham, Tony. (2005)
Plants from the Edge of the World. TIMBER PRESS

Flanagan, Mark, Kirkham, Tony. (2009)
Wilson's China: A Century On. ROYAL BOTANIC GARDENS, KEW

Grimshaw, John, Bayton, Ross, Wilks Hazel. (2009)
New Trees: Recent Introductions to Cultivation.
ROYAL BOTANIC GARDENS, KEW

Hall, Tony. (2018)
The Immortal Yew. ROYAL BOTANIC GARDENS, KEW

Harrison, Christina, Gardiner, Lauren. (2016)
Bizarre Botany. ROYAL BOTANIC GARDENS, KEW

Kirkham, Tony, Harrison, Christina. (2019)
Remarkable Trees. THAMES AND HUDSON

Miles, Archie. (1999)
Silva: The Tree in Britain. EBURY PRESS

Miles, Archie. (2013)
The British Oak. CONSTABLE AND ROBINSON LTD

Miles, Archie. (2006)
The Trees that Made Britain. BBC BOOKS

Pakenham, Thomas. (2015)
Meetings with Remarkable Trees. ORION PUBLISHING CO

Price, Katherine. (2014)
The Kew Guide. ROYAL BOTANIC GARDENS, KEW

Tudge, Colin. (2006)
The Secret Life of Trees: How They Live and Why They Matter.
PENGUIN GROUP

Yamanaka, Masumi, Harrison, Christina, Rix, Martyn. (2015)
Treasured Trees. ROYAL BOTANIC GARDENS, KEW

COVER: *Quercus* x *hispanica* 'Lucombeana' by Andrew McRobb/ © RBG Kew

PHOTO CREDITS: Jeff Eden, Christina Harrison, Paul Little, Andrew McRobb, all © RBG Kew

Second Edition published in 2019
First published in 2008 by
Royal Botanic Gardens, Kew, Richmond, Surrey, TW9 3AE, UK
www.kew.org

Distributed on behalf of the
Royal Botanic Gardens, Kew in North America by the University of Chicago Press,1427 East 60th St, Chicago, IL 60637, USA.

ISBN 978 1 84246 687 2

British Library Cataloguing in Publication Data
A catalogue record for this book is available from the British Library

Printed in Great Britain by Charlesworth Press

For information or to purchase all Kew titles please visit shop.kew.org/kewbooksonline or email publishing@kew.org

Kew's mission is to be the global resource in plant and fungal knowledge and the world's leading botanic garden.

Kew receives approximately one third of its funding from Government through the Department for Environment, Food and Rural Affairs (Defra). All other funding needed to support Kew's vital work comes from members, foundations, donors and commercial activities, including book sales.